HEROES AND WARRIORS
Judas Maccabeus
REBEL OF ISRAEL

MARK HEALY
Plates by RICHARD HOOK

Firebird Books

Also available in this series by the same author:
JOSHUA Conqueror of Canaan
KING DAVID Warlord of Israel
NEBUCHADNEZZAR Scourge of Zion

For Ron and Eileen

Acknowledgements

Many of the quotations herein are taken from *The New Jerusalem Bible* published by Darton Longman & Todd, whose translation and permission are gratefully acknowledged. For information on the military forces, the work of the Wargames Research Group and of the historian B. Bar-Kochva are gratefully acknowledged, and recommended to all readers interested in this period.

First published in the UK 1989 by Firebird Books
P.O. Box 327, Poole, Dorset BH15 2RG

Copyright © 1989 Firebird Books Ltd
Text copyright © 1989 Mark Healy

Distributed in the United States by
Sterling Publishing Co, Inc
Two Park Avenue, New York, NY 10016

Distributed in Australia by
Capricorn Link (Australia) Pty Ltd
P.O. Box 665, Lane Cove, NSW 2066

British Library Cataloguing in Publication Data
Healy, Mark
    Judas Maccabeus: rebel of Israel. – (Heroes and warriors).
    1. Palestine. Maccabees, ancient period.
    I. Title   II. Hook, Richard   III. Series
    933'.009'92
    ISBN 1 85314 011 2

Series editor Stuart Booth
Designed by Kathryn S.A. Booth
Typeset by Inforum Typesetting, Portsmouth
Monochrome origination by Castle Graphics
Colour separations by Kingfisher Facsimile, Frome
Colour printed by Barwell Colour Print Ltd (Midsomer Norton)
Printed and bound in Great Britain at The Bath Press

Juda   eus

THE BATTLES OF JUDAS MACCABEUS

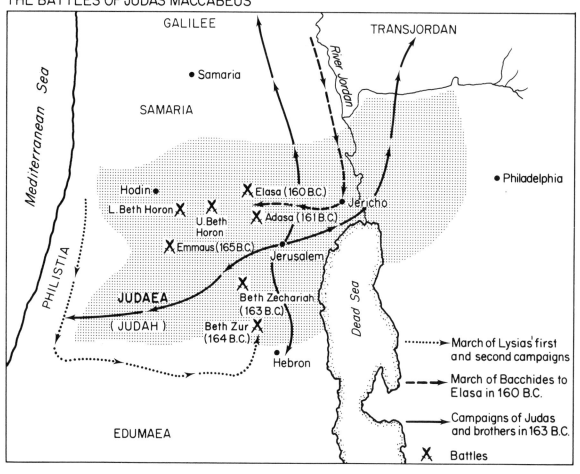

Map shows: GALILEE, TRANSJORDAN, Mediterranean Sea, • Samaria, SAMARIA, River Jordan, • Philadelphia, Hodin •, L.Beth Horon X, U.Beth Horon X, X Elasa (160 B.C.), X Adasa (161 B.C.), Jericho •, X Emmaus (165 B.C.), Jerusalem •, PHILISTIA, JUDAEA (JUDAH), X Beth Zechariah (163 B.C.), Beth Zur (164 B.C.) X, • Hebron, Dead Sea, EDUMAEA

Legend:
• • • • → March of Lysias' first and second campaigns
— — → March of Bacchides to Elasa in 160 B.C.
⟶ Campaigns of Judas and brothers in 163 B.C.
X Battles

4

The man who kept Israel safe . . . the battles he fought, the exploits he performed, and all his titles to greatness have not [all] been recorded; but they were very many.

(1 Maccabees 9:19–22)

Saviour of his People

Few peoples in the world have a history as long as that of the Jews and fewer still can match the centuries of indignity, prejudice, violence and genocide directed against them. Whilst the memory of the Holocaust will never fade, the years have dimmed the knowledge that over two thousand years earlier, a similar policy of persecution was adopted that seemed aimed at nothing less than the anhiliation of the Jewish faith. It was against this backdrop of repression and genocide in the second century B.C. that Judas, the third son of Mattathias and named 'the Hammerer' emerged to save his people.

As is the case for many of the biblical heroes, he is known for his deeds rather than for what we know about him as a person. The notion of biography, of a concern for the personal details of an individual's life deemed so essential by us twentieth century moderns, was a concept alien to the Biblical writers. If such details were included it was frequently almost by 'the slip of the pen' and not deliberately.

In the case of Judas Maccabeus, we have scarcely the skeleton of biography on which to hang the flesh of his career. For a start, we do not even know how old he was when, on the death of his father in 166 B.C., he assumed the leadership of the nascent Jewish rebellion against the forces of the Seleucid empire. Yet though we know nothing definite of his appearance or of any other matters of a personal nature, we can say that he was a remarkable and charismatic figure. Apparently without any professional military experience, he ran roughshod over one of the finest military machines of the ancient world, humbling it by repeated 'hammer blows' that sent it reeling and forever dented its prestige. His battles, particularly those of his early days as a guerrilla fighter, have provided inspiration for many in a similar predicament down the ages. Indeed, when the British soldier Orde Wingate, later the founder of the Chindits, was defending Zionist settlers in Palestine in the 1930s, he used the accounts of Judas' battles in the *First* and *Second Books of Maccabees* to help plan his 'penetration' method of light infantry operations.

It is therefore in his deeds that we must look for Judas Maccabeus. The *First Book of Maccabees* is in no doubt as to the stature of the man:

He extended the fame of his people.
Like a giant, he put on the breastplate
and buckled on his war harness;
he engaged in battle after battle,
protecting the ranks with his sword.
He was like a young lion roaring over its prey
He pursued and tracked down the renegades,
he consigned those who troubled his people to the flames.
The renegades quailed with the terror he inspired
all evil doers were utterly confounded,
and deliverance went forward under his leadership.
He brought bitterness to many a king
and rejoicing to Jacob by his deeds,
His memory is blessed for ever and ever.

(1 Maccabees 3:3–7)

Crucial to an understanding of his deeds and times is some insight into the relationship between Hellenism and Judaism in the period prior to the Jewish revolt of 166 B.C. In the clash between these two seemingly incompatible cultures, and in the struggle of the Jews to assert and retain their religious and cultural identity in the face of the threat of Hellenism, lay the roots of the brutal conflict that brought forth Judas Maccabeus as the saviour of his people.

Hellenism and Judaism

When Alexander the Great died in Babylon on 10 June, 323 B.C. he bequeathed as his legacy an empire that stretched from Greece to the borders of India. The Diadochi – his successors, former generals and brothers in arms – dismembered his creation shortly after his death, and attempted to carve out their own kingdoms. Nevertheless, the cities he founded, his greatest legacy to the lands he conquered, remained. Plutarch speaks of as many as seventy, and it was in these cities that Greek culture or Hellenism was perpetuated throughout the lands of the conquest.

In Palestine, both the Ptolemies, who ruled the area between 301 and 198 B.C., and the Seleucids who succeeded them, founded many cities. These were either founded as new 'Greek' cities, with a core of Greek and Macedonian settlers, or were older settlements taken over and converted to Greek ways.

Under Antiochus III, known as 'the Great', Palestine passed under the power of the Seleucid monarchy, along with many territories in the east that were annexed in the great drive to rebuild the empire. An attempt to match this conquest in the west resulted in catastrophe at Magnesia in 190 B.C., when Antiochus was decisively defeated by the Romans.

Conflict of Cultures

The Greek language itself served as a vehicle for the transmission of Hellenistic attitudes and values. Even the Jews were not immune to the attractions of Hellenistic thought, with many forsaking the traditions of their fathers.

Yet to the traditionalists, who were critical of the new attitudes, true religion was embodied in the Torah – the first five books of the Old Testament, containing the 613 Commandments of the Law given to Moses at Sinai by God. Divine revelation had imparted to the Jewish people the true religion and the commandments to set themselves apart and have no other gods. Thus, the compromise that those in high places effected by embracing Hellenism – even though their motives had little to do with religion and much more to do with the amassing of wealth and political power – was perceived by many as a dagger aimed at the very heart of Judaism.

Seleucus IV Philopator succeeded to the Seleucid throne on the death of Antiochus III in 187 B.C. His abortive attempt to seize the Temple treasury in Jerusalem was prompted by the need to pay the crippling war indemnity imposed by the Romans at Apamea. He was assassinated by his chief minister Heliodorus in 175 B.C.

Thus it was a small, but powerful element in Jerusalem that attempted to make the population of Judaea adopt Hellenistic culture. That opposition to these pro-Hellenists was already evolving cannot be doubted, but it was not until the accession of Antiochus IV to the Seleucid throne in 175 B.C. and the adoption of his policies that the spark of growing antagonism was fanned into open rebellion.

The Mad King

Antiochus IV was the third son of Antiochus III, king of the Seleucid realm in Palestine. At an early age he had acquired a profound admiration for the institutions and policies of the Romans. This was a consequence of some fifteen years spent as their 'guest', when, following the defeat of Antiochus III at the Battle of Magnesia in 190 B.C., the young Antiochus had been sent to Rome to serve as hostage for his father. Those years had a profound effect on him. In 175 B.C., his elder brother, Seleucus IV, was required by Rome to exchange Antiochus as hostage with his second son Demetrius. Freed, the ardent young Hellenist travelled to Athens, returning with an almost evangelical commitment to the concept and spread of Hellenism. This single-mindedness, which verged on the obsessional, allied to his irrational nature, moved some to play on the name of his royal title, adopted in 169 B.C., of 'Theos Epiphanes' meaning 'God Manifest' and change it to 'Epimanes' meaning 'the Mad'.

In Athens, Antiochus cultivated a wide circle of friends and was appointed chief magistrate. Then he learned that the King's chief minister Heliodorus had brought about the assassination of his brother Seleucus IV. With the assistance of King Eumenes II of Pergamum, he therefore returned to Antioch determined to overthrow the usurper. Within a short time Heliodorus was killed and Antiochus was crowned king. All of this took place despite the fact that his nephew Demetrius was still a hostage in Rome and was the rightful heir to the throne. The consequences were to be far reaching, with Demetrius playing an important role in future events.

A passionate advocate of Hellenism, Antiochus IV sought to propogate and impose his views on his realm. His cruel and vindictive campaign against Judaism was designed to suppress all in Judaea who held beliefs he perceived as antagonistic to royal authority. This repression caused the Jewish rebellion and the emergence of Judas the Hammer.

The New Ruler

The empire that Antiochus inherited from his elder brother was in a terrible state. Many of its lands were in danger of breaking away or of being seized by other powers bent on exploiting Seleucid weakness. This weakness arose mainly from the desperate financial state of the Empire. The crippling war indemnity that Rome had imposed on Antiochus III after the Battle of Magnesia severely restricted the capacity of the Seleucid rulers to pay for armies, not only to control the lands they held but also to engage in expansion abroad. In order to fund their armies both Antiochus III and Seleucus IV had embarked on a policy of robbing temples and shrines to obtain cash. Indeed, Antiochus III met his death in the temple of Baal, near Susa in Persia, whilst levying tribute in 187 B.C. However, such a predatory policy did not always succeed. It was the abortive attempt by Seleucus IV to lay his hands on the Temple treasury in Jerusalem that contributed to the unstable situation in Judaea.

Dealing with the Realm

By 173 B.C. Antiochus had repaid the final amount outstanding to Rome and was able to deal with the internal and external problems facing his Empire. He embarked upon a deliberate policy of Hellenisation, to bring a much greater degree of coherence and order to the Empire. Simultaneously, he intended to deal with each of his enemies in turn.

He began with Egypt, for the Ptolemies of Egypt and the Seleucids had been rivals for centuries, with Palestine frequently their theatre of war. But both now had to accede to the will of Rome, the new dominant power in the Eastern Mediterranean.

By the time that Antiochus invaded Egypt for the second time in 168 B.C., he had well and truly incurred the wrath of the Roman Senate. A Roman delegation landed in Eleusis – a suburb of the city of Alexandria, outside of which Antiochus and his army were camped – to meet him and to reveal the extent of Rome's power even in the late second century B.C.

Frustration of Humiliation

The Roman ambassador, Gaius Popillius Laenas, presented himself to the King. After a few pleasantries he produced an ultimatum from the Senate, demanding that Antiochus abandon Egypt forthwith. Taken aback, the Seleucid king asked for some time to consult with his generals and advisers, all of whom were present to witness the treatment of their king. In reply, Popillius Laenas took his walking stick and, dragging it along the ground, inscribed a circle in the dust with Antiochus at its middle. He then demanded an unequivocal answer from Antiochus before he stepped from the circle.

There can be few instances in history where a military power with the symbols of its might all too visible and available has caved in totally to the threat posed by another power. There have been even fewer occasions where a monarch with pretensions to greatness – or even divinity – has been so thoroughly and completely humiliated.

The action was supremely calculated; Antiochus acceded to the Roman demand without demur. He knew what Rome could do – he had seen it for himself at Magnesia and he had no desire to court disaster. However, Seleucid dominion over Coele-Syria was confirmed so at least the King could return, assured of the integrity of the southern part of his realm, albeit 'in high dudgeon indeed and groaning in spirit, but yielding to the necessities of the time'.

The elephant was used extensively in war by the Seleucid forces and frequently appeared on the reverse of coins as the symbol of power. So prestigious was this symbol that it was used by Seleucid kings many years after the animals themselves were no longer employed by their armies.

The consequences of this deep humiliation were profound. Perhaps in another man the humiliation, although still deeply felt, would have been accepted; but this was Antiochus Epiphanes and many feared for the outcome.

He was a man of unpredictable moods. One moment he could be friendly and the next silent and brooding. His behaviour could be quite bizarre, and Polybius, who is a good anecdotal source, writes of him behaving in a quite Neronian manner, carousing with workmen and frequenting public baths, appearing on stage as an actor or taking part in dancing. However, the whimsy could change in a moment to a mood that was dark and threatening and which could manifest itself in cruel and fearfully vindictive behaviour almost obsessional in its desire to expend itself on an object, person or a people.

It was exactly the wrong time for a revolt in Jerusalem led by a renegade attempting to win back the office of High Priest from the Seleucid nominee. Antiochus chose to interpret the revolt as an act of rebellion and in doing so provided for himself the very means whereby he could, at a fearful cost, exorcise the frustrating humiliation inflicted upon his royal person by Gaius Popillius Laenas and the Senate of Rome.

Antiochus and the High Priests

When Antiochus IV had assumed the Seleucid kingship in 175 B.C., the Jews in Judaea were still living according to the decree promulgated by Antiochus III. Thereby, they were free to live according to their ancestral laws. However, the growing influence of Hellenism and the desire of many to see Judaism change to accommodate the 'new' way of thinking, led to a growing conflict over who was to be High Priest in Jerusalem.

The role of High Priest was at once both religious and political. As head of the Jewish religion, he commanded great religious prestige and was responsible for overseeing the cultus in the Temple in Jerusalem. In political terms, he was the figure to whom the Seleucid King spoke about matters of policy. It was in essence a position of great influence and power, and it was this power that was coveted by a number of priestly families strongly sympathetic to Hellenism and the Seleucids.

The High Priest in office at the time of Antiochus' accession was Onias III who held the office between 190 and 174 B.C. He was regarded by his supporters as one who remained faithful to the Law. Politically, he was hostile – albeit very diplomatically – to the Seleucids. Shortly before the death of Seleucus IV he was summoned to Antioch to account for an outbreak of violence in the city between the opposing factions and he was there when the King was assassinated.

Bribery and Corruption

Soon after seizing power in 175 B.C., Antiochus dismissed Onias and appointed a new High Priest by the name of Jason. This action by the King set a doubtful precedent; the appointment of a new High Priest had always been regarded as an internal matter for the Jews. It did not bode well for the future, for Jason had secured the position 'with a promise of three hundred and sixty talents of silver, with eighty talents to come from some other source of revenue'. Given the appetite of the Seleucid kings for money, Antiochus could hardly resist such an offer.

In order to ingratiate himself even further with the new King and to demonstrate his commitment to Hellenism, Jason then offered the King more money in return for permission to build in Jerusalem a sports centre (gymnasium) and training centre (ephebia) to impart and instil the spirit of Hellenism in the young men of the city. He further petitioned that Jerusalem and its inhabitants enjoy the same privileges as those of Antioch and be known as 'Antiochenes'. Jason was certainly not acting unilaterally in this matter. Supporting him were a group of powerful pro-Hellenists from the priestly class, as well as businessmen and merchants who hoped to benefit economically from much closer ties with the Seleucid regime.

Three years later a certain Menelaus, emulating the example set by Jason some years before, offered Antiochus 300 talents more than Jason had sent to Antioch as tribute for the King. In his turn Jason was deposed and Menelaus made High Priest. Rather than await the return of Menelaus and certain death Jason fled the city to the Trans-Jordan.

Ruthless Repression

Within a short while, however, Menelaus was in difficulty. Not only did he experience great problems in fulfilling his financial promise to the King, but of greater significance was the growing opposition to him as High Priest. Finally, insurrection broke out in the city, causing Antiochus to divert his army to Jerusalem on his return from Egypt, in order to re-assert order.

He then ordered his soldiers to cut down without mercy everyone they encountered, and to butcher all who took refuge in their houses. It was a

As head of the Jewish religion, the High Priest occupied a prestigious position of both religious and political power.

10

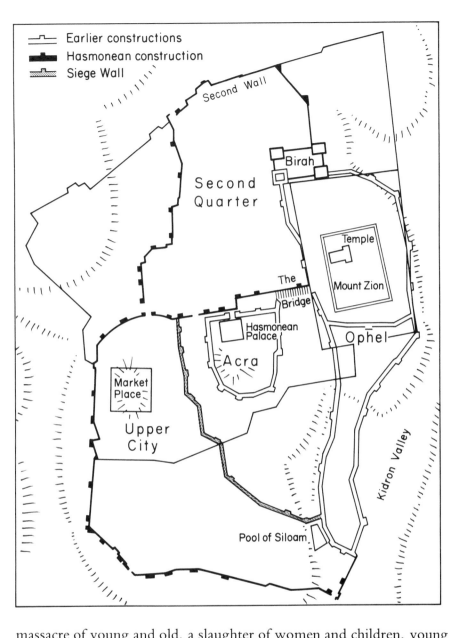

Legend:
- Earlier constructions
- Hasmonean construction
- Siege Wall

Second Wall

Birah

Second Quarter

Temple

Mount Zion

The Bridge

Hasmonean Palace

Ophel

Acra

Market Place

Upper City

Kidron Valley

Pool of Siloam

massacre of young and old, a slaughter of women and children, young girls and infants. There were eighty thousand victims in the course of three days, forty thousand dying by violence and as many again being sold into slavery.

Antiochus then pillaged the Temple, even stripping the gold plate from the façade, with the help of Menelaus and finally returned to Antioch with his booty. He left behind him in charge of the military garrison in the city a Phrygian by the name of Philip who was plainly a very ruthless individual. His brief was to prop up the rule of Menelaus with Seleucid troops.

Main features of Jerusalem during the time of the Maccabeans. Of significance is the size of the Akra (or Acra) built during the reign of Antiochus IV to house the Seleucid garrison and as a refuge for the Hellenising Jews. Judas laid seige to it unsuccessfully during the winter of 163–162 B.C.

In 168 B.C., following a rumour that Antiochus had been killed on campaign in Egypt, Jason hired a thousand mercenaries and returned to Jerusalem with the intention of reclaiming the office of High Priest. Entering the city they began their own massacre of the people in what seems to have been a senseless orgy of blood letting. The only effect was the alienation of those in the city who may have supported him against Menelaus. Driven from the city Jason went into exile and finally died in Sparta.

Once more word reached Antiochus of trouble in Jerusalem. Again he assumed it to be a rebellion, this time sending the Mysarch Apollonius with an army of 22,000 men. Apollonius waited until the Sabbath. Then, taking advantage of the Jews as they rested from work, he ordered his men to parade fully armed. All who came to watch were put to the sword. He next rushed into the city with his armed troops, and cut down an immense number of its population. On the orders of the King, the walls of the city were then dismantled and a heavily fortified base was constructed within the city. This served as a base for the garrison troops and also functioned as a kind of Greek political office, with its own institutions providing a centre within the city for the Hellenising party to continue their activities.

Judaism as the Enemy

The most sinister of the King's decrees was that which stated 'that all were to become a single people, each nation renouncing its particular customs'.

Having realised that opposition to him in Judaea was firmly rooted in the Jewish religion, Antiochus' solution to the political problem of control was to order that Judaism be proscribed. Specifically, the decree was not issued throughout the whole Seleucid Empire, but only in Judaea and directed at the Jews of that province.

With the decree began the great travail of the Jewish people. Paradoxically, this policy of enforced Hellenisation was to achieve not a quiescent people who had repudiated the faith of their fathers, but a rebellion perceived by the Jews as a battle against the forces of darkness, the consequences of which were to change the face of Judaism.

Persecution and Revolt

In the wake of the decree announcing that all 'were to become a single people', Antiochus took steps to end the ancestral worship of the Jewish people in Judaea. In all these matters he was supported by the pro-Hellenists amongst the Jews and it was with their active help that the policy against the Jewish religion in Judaea began. Yet, in the scope of the persecution were displayed a vindictiveness and cruelty which arose

A notable innovation by Antiochus IV was the conversion of some 5,000 guard infantry – the argyraspides – into heavy troops. Apart from the retention of the Thracian helmet they were armed and equipped as Roman triarii. They protected the elephants at Beth-Zechariah and equipped with pilum and scutum, had a greater degree of flexibility than the traditional Seleucid phalanx.

directly from the personality of the King. In abrogating the charter granted to the Jews by Antiochus III in 198 B.C. (in which the Law of Moses was recognised as Jewish civil law) and by re-imposing gentile practices in their place, to disobey the King's commands on these matters was made synonymous with political rebellion. Thus, to live as a gentile and disavow Jewish practices became the measure of loyalty to the Seleucid state.

Accounts are quite explicit as to the content and consequences of the King's policy:

> The king sent edicts by messenger to Jerusalem and the towns of Judah, directing them to adopt customs foreign to the country, banning burnt offerings, sacrifices and libations from the sanctuary, profaning Sabbaths and feasts, defiling the sanctuary and everything holy, building altars, shrines and temples for idols, sacrificing pigs and unclean beasts, leaving their sons uncircumcised and prostituting themselves to all kinds of impurity and abomination, so that they should forget the Law and revoke all observance of it. Anyone not obeying the king's command was to be put to death.
>
> (1 Maccabees 1:44–50)

As a test of their loyalty to his person and the Seleucid state, Antiochus Epiphanes had decreed that all the Jews within Judaea must sacrifice to an image like this of the Greek god Zeus, or die.

The greatest of all the abominations in the eyes of those who opposed Hellenism was the setting up on the Temple altar of an image dedicated to Olympian Zeus which bore the features of Antiochus Epiphanes himself. On this, swine's flesh was sacrificed, an act which illustrates the depth of the hatred and vindictiveness that must have inspired this persecution. Even the Greeks were not in the habit of sacrificing pigs to Zeus – this was a very special humiliation reserved, it would seem, for the Jews.

Atrocity of Repression

Many atrocities were inflicted by the Seleucid forces on the worthy people who chose death rather than forsake the Law. For example, two Jewish women were charged with having circumcised their children. They were paraded round the town, with their babies at their breasts, and then hurled over the city wall.

But perhaps no account of faith in the face of persecution is more famous than the account in the *Second Book of Maccabees* 7 which describes how a mother witnessed the martyrdom of her seven sons in a most appalling manner. Yet she comforted them with the injunction, which is one of the main theological concerns of the book, that God would not stand by and witness the persecution of his chosen people but would bring judgement on those who were the instigators of such horror and persecution.

Seeds of Revolt

Thus, it was the personality of Antiochus Epiphanes and his idiosyncratic policies that finally provided the catalyst for the Jews of Judaea to translate a growing hostility to Hellenism into armed rebellion. From the ruthless and pitiless religious persecution directed towards nothing less than the total extirpation of the faith of their fathers, there emerged a war in which there could be no quarter given on either side. But it was not amongst the people of the great city that the rebellion began; it was from the hill country to the north-west of Jerusalem that the avenger of Israel was to appear.

Fire of Rebellion

The spark that ignited the flame of revolt in Judaea was the enforcement of the royal decree that all should show their loyalty to the King by swearing allegiance to his name – and to the cause he espoused. Antiochus despatched commissioners from the major centres to the outlying towns and villages. Supported by a small detachment of troops, one of these Seleucid officials journeyed from Jerusalem to Modein, a village situated in the hill country to the north-west of the city and close to the modern Israeli town of Lod. There they were to demand that the Jews, as was being required all over Judaea, make sacrifices to Dionysus and Olympian Zeus as token of their allegiance to Antiochus Epiphanes. The tactics employed by these officials were to search out the leading citizens of each area with a view to getting them to publicly acquiesce in the test of loyalty so that others, seeing their example, would follow suit. Seemingly some did indeed succumb, seduced by the bribe of being declared 'A King's Friend', a title which gave the recipient certain privileges. It was for this reason that the unnamed Seleucid commissioner sent word to the leading family of the district to present themselves at the altar already set up for the sacrifice in the middle of the town.

Calling together his five sons, Mattathias, son of Simeon and a priest of the line of Joarib, made his way to the centre of the village where a large crowd of Jews had gathered to both witness and partake in the sacrifice. Although Mattathias and his sons – John, Simon, Judas, Eleazar and Jonathan – deliberately distanced themselves from the crowd, it was to him that the Seleucid official turned first to speak:

You are a respected leader, a great man in this town; you have sons and brothers to support you. Be the first to step forward and conform to the King's decree, as all nations have done, and the leaders of Judah and the survivors in Jerusalem; you and your sons shall be reckoned among the Friends of the King, you and your sons will be honoured with gold and silver and many presents.

(1 Maccabees 2:17–18)

Plainly, the Seleucid official did not know the mettle of the man with whom he was dealing, for Mattathias' reply was unambiguous in its absolute rejection of any compromise with the decree of Antiochus:

Even if every nation living in the king's dominions obeys him, each forsaking his ancestral religion to conform to his decrees, I, my sons and my brothers will still follow the covenant of our ancestors. May heaven preserve us from forsaking the Law and its observances. As for the king's orders, we will not follow them: we shall not swerve from our own religion either to the right or to the left.

(1 Maccabees 2:19–23)

Such a reply carried a death sentence not only for Mattathias but also for his sons and kinsmen, but unlike many others of his people he was not prepared to go as a lamb to the slaughter on the blade of a gentile. Within a moment of Mattathias uttering his reply, a Jew stepped forward from the crowd with the offer that he be the first to sacrifice on the altar. This so angered Mattathias that he threw himself on the man and slaughtered him on the altar. So Antiochus Epiphanes did receive a sacrifice from Mattathias; not the one demanded but another, a human one, that of an apostate Jew!

The Cause is Born

Very quickly Mattathias and his sons fell on the surprised official and his bodyguard. Recognising the inevitable consequences of what seems to have been a completely spontaneous action, Mattathias determined that this was to be the beginning of his revolt against the Seleucid King. He proceeded to go through the town shouting out at the top of his voice: 'Let everyone who has any zeal for the Law and takes his stand on the covenant come out and follow me' (1 *Maccabees* 2:27).

Fleeing from Modein, Mattathias and his sons and followers escaped to the Gophna hills and esconced themselves in the area around the Beth-Horon Pass. From there they started to wage a guerrilla campaign against the Seleucid forces in the area.

It was while they were in these hills that news reached them of a massacre of their co-religionists in the desert by Seleucid forces. Apparently the group of Jews had been tracked down and surrounded in the caves in which they were sheltering. Refusing to surrender and refusing to fight on the grounds that it was the Sabbath and that fighting could be construed as work and thus forbidden by God's ordinance, they had chosen to die. The Seleucid forces broke into the caves, and the attack pressed home. Over 1000 Jews were slaughtered, with their wives, children and cattle.

As a consequence Mattathias, in his capacity as priest, ordered that fighting on the Sabbath was permitted if necessary to save 'the Law' and those who fought to protect it.

Freedom Fighters

The growing ruthlessness of the Seleucid response and the news of Mattathias' stand at Modein inspired many to flock to his cause. Of all those who did, none were more important than the Hasidim or 'pious ones'. That many of these Hasidim – 'each one a volunteer on the side of the Law' – were poor and from rural backgrounds lent an overtone of class conflict to the revolt. The rebellion very rapidly began to assume the characteristics of an all out ideological conflict, with no quarter being given by either side. With his rapidly growing body of guerrilla soldiers, Mattathias began to sweep through the hill country around Jerusalem. In

In the early days of their revolt, the Jewish guerrilla forces were simply armed. The sling was a weapon of some pedigree in their hands and wreaked fearful havoc amongst the Seleucid troops in the narrow defiles of the Judaean hills.

those areas where the Seleucid forces were unable, by virtue of the geography, to maintain more than a token presence or control, he 'cleansed' villages and towns of the trappings of the enemy. It is possible to see in the mind's eye an image of the descent from the hills, perhaps at night, and the rounding up of those deemed to be ideologically unsound. Their names procured perhaps by denunciation as collaborators, their ruthless despatch served as an example to others not to succumb to the entreaties and bribes of the enemy. Certainly the methods of ideologically motivated guerrillas, be they of a religious or political orientation, have varied little over the course of nearly two thousand years. Only the instruments with which they deal with the enemy have changed; whether one is despatched by a sword or a Kalashnikov matters little to the one who has slipped into untruth! Certainly there is nothing in the text to suggest that the ruthlessness with which Mattathias, and later Judas, eliminated those 'hostile' to the Law was thought to be wrong. On the contrary, it is condoned as the necessary means whereby zeal for the Law is made manifest in response to the dire circumstances facing the Jews. The methods were thus appropriate to the nature of the problem, for to Mattathias and his followers there could be no compromise with this enemy:

Mattathias and his friends made a tour, overthrowing the altars and forcibly circumcising all the boys they found uncircumcised in the territories of Israel. They hunted down the upstarts and managed their campaign to good effect. They wrested the Law out of the control of the gentiles and the kings and reduced the sinners to impotence.

(1 *Maccabees* 2:45–48)

Judas the Hammerer

Already old in years at the time of his revolt against Antiochus Epiphanes and realising that the exertions of campaigning had taken their toll, Mattathias knew that his death was approaching. He summoned his sons to give them his final instructions and restated what was, in essence, one of the theological themes of the *First Book of Maccabees*:

This is the time, my children, for you to have a burning zeal for the Law and to give your lives for the covenant of our ancestors.

He then asked his sons to look to their brother Simon for wise council, but in more immediate matters to follow their third brother Judas, who had already demonstrated such a remarkable prowess in war. It was to him they must look in their fight with the forces of Antiochus Epiphanes, for in him Mattathias had seen the abilities of one who could realise with a vengeance his dying words that they 'Pay back the Gentiles to the full, and hold fast to the ordinances of the Law'.

Thus it was that from the death of his father in 166 B.C. to his own demise on the battlefield of Elasa some six years later, Judas, nicknamed Maccabeus meaning the 'Hammerer', played out his short but remarkable career as the defender of the faith of his people. In that brief period of

First victory of the guerrilla army of Judas Maccabeus. Having defeated a Seleucid force in the mountains, Judas took as booty the sword of Apollonius, the dead enemy commander, and wore it to the end of his days.

time he was to humble the armies of one of the most powerful states of the day on a number of occasions, using methods that became the inspiration of many a guerrilla fighter to this day.

Guerrilla Warrior

It is apparent from the half-hearted response of the Seleucid forces to the activities of Mattathias that they did not perceive, at first, the rebellious Jewish forces to be a real threat to their control of Judaea. This arose partly from the understandable view of the professional Seleucid soldiery, battle hardened as they were by their wars against the armies of the Ptolemies, Romans and Parthians, that an ill-equipped and, to their mind, poorly led band of religious fanatics could hardly pose a serious military threat to their power on the field of battle. In fact, the Seleucids really had little if any experience of the type of warfare that Judas, son of Mattathias now brought to bear. Guerrilla warfare is of its very nature unconventional and is dependent for its success on factors with which the professional soldiery of the day were not trained to cope.

The genius of Judas lay in his almost intuitive selection of the field of battle. He almost invariably was able to choose a site that by its very nature would negate whatever advantages the enemy had and accentuate the few material and moral qualities his own forces possessed. When on ground and at a time of his own choosing Judas Maccabeus showed – as did many others who emulated his example after him – that a guerrilla force led and inspired by a great cause could defeat a much better trained and equipped conventional army.

Strategy of Struggle

We can best understand how Judas deployed his forces or organised his guerrilla army by looking at modern guerrilla warfare, which would seem in essence to be little different to that waged by Judas. We can infer a number of things without which it certainly would not have been possible for him to fight at all.

Firstly, he must have had an extensive supply of intelligence with respect to the Seleucid forces. This was helped by the fact that they were concentrated as garrison forces in the larger towns and could easily be kept under surveillance. As is usually the case in guerrilla warfare there were many amongst the population who, whilst not willing to fight themselves, were only too happy to pass on information to Judas' camp in the mountains. This would imply that Judas was fighting for an objective that had the support of the majority of the Jewish people in Judaea. When, over twenty centuries later, Mao-Tse-Tung was to formulate the basis of successful guerrilla warfare, in stating that guerrilla

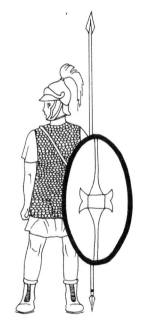

In early battles, the heaviest Seleucid troops encountered by the guerrilla fighters were probably curassiers or 'Thorakites' used to support the light infantry in the hill country. From their stripped bodies, Maccabean soldiers acquired as booty much of their weaponry and mail armour.

After defeating Lysias at Beth-Zur, Judas returned to Jerusalem, where in December 164 B.C. the Temple was cleansed and rededicated with great jubilation. The event is celebrated to this day in the Festival of Hanukkah.

warfare was bound to fail without any political goal or if its political objectives did not coincide with the hopes of the people so that their sympathy, cooperation and assistance could not be gained.

At this very early stage of his leadership of the rebellion Judas would not have seen his cause in stark political terms, but more as a fight for religious freedom. Nevertheless, rapidly he came to realise that such religious freedom could not be sustained without the Jews securing their political independence, free from the domination of any foreign power.

It is clear that, despite the general support of the population, food and provisions were frequently in short supply in the rebel camp and hunger and exhaustion were their constant companions. Prior to the attack on the forces of Seron his men complained to Judas: 'How can we, few as we are, engage such numbers? We are exhausted as it is, not having had anything to eat today'.

We must also assume that in the early days of the rebellion the Jewish forces were poorly equipped, with the main weaponry being slings, bows and arrows, some spears and swords, and an endless supply of heavy rocks as hand projectiles. However, even this 'poor' arsenal in the hands of men with both the skill to employ such weaponry and the will to succeed can effect tremendous casualties when employed in the right conditions. In the early days that was where the guerrilla warfare of Judas Maccabeus paid dividends. Later, when attempting to take on the Seleucid forces on ground more suited to the type of warfare that was their métier, the lack of real training of the Maccabean forces led to their defeat in the full-scale, pitched battles. Nevertheless, the nature of the Seleucid forces – with their baggage trains and conventional marching order – required them to make transit through Judaea using the main ways. These frequently took them through the valleys and narrow defiles which were the perfect places for Judas to launch his attacks. It was in such circumstances that he was to realise his first victories.

The Sword of Apollonius

It was shortly after Judas assumed the leadership of the rebel forces that the first Seleucid moves were directed against him. A force was raised by Apollonius, the governor of Samaria, who, the year previously, had been despatched by Antiochus to collect tribute from the towns of Judaea. As on that occasion, he was again supported by mercenaries from Mysia – auxiliary light infantry with a scattering of light cavalry troopers.

Moving out from Samaria, the Seleucid force struck south into the forbidding hills which ran across the route to Jerusalem. Somewhere along their path Judas launched his attack.

Forewarned, probably from the moment of their departure, Judas had ample time to pick the place for his ambush. Although we have no real details about this battle, we can assume it took place in a defile and in a

Senior Seleucid officers of the army of Antiochus IV wore rich apparel and provide the likely appearance of Apollonius when he met his death at the hands of Judas Maccabeus in 166 A.D.

terrain where the Seleucid forces would have found it almost impossible to defend themselves against a fusillade of sling stones as they scrambled for what little cover could be found. Under a deluge of rocks, arrows and stones, the numbers of the Seleucid troops would probably have been depleted considerably before Judas gave the order to descend into the defile itself to finish them off.

With the ancient Jewish battle cry of 'Sword of the Lord' on their lips, the Maccabean fighters came down from the heights and rapidly despatched the remaining Seleucid soldiery. The few survivors – probably those at the rear of the line – managed to escape and returned with news of the disaster that had overtaken Apollonius and his men. For Judas the victory was of double benefit; spoils were seized from the dead Seleucid soldiers and Judas himself took the sword of Apollonius, a weapon he used throughout his life. For a guerrilla army, the abandoned weapons of the enemy are always the single most important source for the re-equipment of their own limited arsenal – and no doubt the sword Judas 'liberated' from Apollonius was a finely wrought and personalised weapon as befitting a man of his importance. Such acquisitions were vital, for within a short while another expedition, albeit again somewhat limited, was mounted by the Seleucids to wipe out Judas and his men.

It is clear from reports of these early Seleucid responses that the bulk of the troops stationed in the provinces of Samaria and Judaea were mercenaries of indifferent quality. This meant that Judas was not faced with the superior soldiery that comprised the main Seleucid army. The morale of the enemy facing him was probably considerably lower than that of the professional Seleucid army whom he later fought. Thus their stability in battle, particularly under the detrimental conditions Judas forced upon them, certainly reduced their ability or desire to withstand the Maccabean attacks.

Defeat of Seron

As with Apollonius, the second attempt to destroy Judas' growing guerrilla army was a unilateral decision by Seron, a middle-ranking Seleucid official, determined to lead a successful expedition and so gain kudos in the eyes of his superiors. The clear inference is that neither the officials in Jerusalem nor Antiochus himself took the threat of Judas seriously, or had heard of him as yet. It would seem that the Seleucid force moved southwards from Seron's base in Coele-Syria, approximately to southern Phoenicia, following the coastal route and then swung inland through Judaea. They intended to march through the pass at Beth-Horon, one of the traditional invasion routes into the Judaean hills, but it was here that Judas decided to attack.

There were, in fact, two places of that name: one a 'Lower' and the other an 'Upper' Beth-Horon located at the top of the pass. The place was one of some pedigree in the history of the Jewish people for it was in

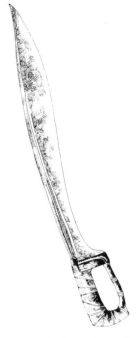

The Book of Maccabees *tells how Judas took the sword from the body of Apollonius and wore it throughout his life. The kopis, a single-edged slashing sword, was popular throughout the Greco–Roman world at this time. One belonging to a superior officer such as Apollonius would have been ornate and personalised.*

The Seleucid armies made extensive use of mercenary soldiers like this Arab mounted on a camel and with his 6-foot long sword.

this pass that in the thirteenth century B.C. Joshua with the 'help' of the Lord defeated the five kings of the Amorites.

Judas chose to lay an ambush near the highest point of the pass. Having struggled up the pass, heavily laden with their supplies and equipment, the Seleucid soldiers would be tired. They would also be strung out along the length of the pass and not at all prepared for battle with their arms and equipment packed up for travelling. Furthermore, Judas would no doubt have been aware that for the leading elements the sight of the top of the pass would have led them, quite naturally, to think in terms of rest and relief from the strenuous exertions of the ascent; psychologically, therefore, they were totally unprepared for battle. Judas realised that the attack had to be on the van of the Seleucid force because his men were not in a good state for battle. We have already mentioned their shortage of food and supplies so Judas was depending upon panic and desperation spreading down the Seleucid line to cause as much injury to the enemy as his attack.

Having addressed his men – chiding them for their fear of the number of the enemy and declaring that 'Heaven accords the strength', he made a sudden sally against Seron and his force. Overwhelming them, Judas pursued the enemy down from Beth-Horon as far as the plain, killing about 800 whilst the rest took refuge 'in the country of the Philistines'. No doubt in their haste to escape, the Seleucid force abandoned all their weapons and supplies. This was counted a great blessing.

The outcome of Judas' success and growing reputation was that for the first time more than token Seleucid forces were sent against him – for the first time his skills on the battlefield and as a leader of men were to be tested in the face of a full-scale battle against a Seleucid army.

The King Strikes Back

It was while he was campaigning in the east against the Parthians during the autumn of 165 B.C. that news of the two defeats inflicted on his forces in Judaea was deemed to be of sufficient importance for Antiochus himself to be informed. There is no suggestion that this rebellion was thought dangerous enough to require him to abandon the Parthian campaign.

Whilst recognising the need to re-establish order in Judaea and suppress the armed rebellion, he apparently felt that this could be achieved by others while he devoted himself to the much more important and lucrative eastern campaign needed to fill the depleted royal coffers. He thus sent word to his chancellor Lysias, both his representative at Antioch and the guardian of his son (the future Antiochus V Eupator), to raise an army and then despatch it to Judaea to quash the revolt.

Seleucid light cavalry trooper equipped with javelin, shield and Thracian helmet. Gorgias left his camp at night with a force of infantry equipped like this in the hope of catching Judas Maccabeus and his men asleep in their camp.

The Army Advances

To command the army, Lysias chose Ptolemy, a professional soldier and general in charge of Seleucid forces in Coele-Syria and Phoenicia; but he devolved the leadership of the actual campaign to Nicanor, son of Patroclus, who was one of the King's 'Close Friends'. He in turn appointed an experienced general by the name of Gorgias to command the army. Obviously a man after the King's heart, Nicanor suggested raising tribute by the sale of Jewish prisoners of war. He lost no time in sending to the seaboard towns an invitation to come and buy Jewish manpower.

The size of the Seleucid army that the *First Book of Maccabees* (3:39) speaks of as advancing on Judaea is plainly in error, a result of the common tendency of ancient writers to exaggerate. Thus we are presented with the claim that Lysias 'despatched forty thousand foot and seven thousand cavalry to invade the land of Judah'. Whereas in the *Second Book of Maccabees* (8:9) the writer speaks of a smaller force comprising at least twenty thousand men.

Whilst other figures given in the *Second Book of Maccabees* for the forces engaged in battles are greatly exaggerated, the figure of at least 20,000 men is reasonable in this case. Certainly, Bar Kochva in his study of the Seleucid army thinks that a figure in excess of 20,000 men, including locally recruited Edomaean and Philistine mercenary auxiliaries, is likely. The much larger figure given in the *First Book of Maccabees* and quoted above means that such a force would have comprised the bulk of the army Antiochus displayed at Daphne in 166 B.C. (46,000 foot

It was along the pass separating the two settlements of Lower Beth-Horon (above) and Upper Beth-Horon that Judas triumphed over Seron's Seleucid forces. Catching them strung out over the length of the pass, his attack on the head of the enemy column produced panic and fear down its entire length. There were many Seleucid casualties.

soldiers, including a Macedonian phalanx of 20,000 men, 8,500 cavalry and 36 or 42 elephants). But as we have already stated, the main elements of this army were ear-marked by Antiochus for the much more important campaign against the Parthians. Thus, the writer of the *First Book of Maccabees* cannot be correct in suggesting that Antiochus left half of his troops to deal with the Jewish rebellion. It is simply a case of the official historian of the House of Hasmon exaggerating numbers in order to show Judas Maccabeus in an even more favourable light.

When the news of the size of this Seleucid force reached Judaea, together with information about their intentions towards the Jewish population, there was understandable trepidation. Even Judas and his brothers saw the situation as going from bad to worse.

The Seleucid army, having advanced southwards, encamped at Emmaus and being, it seems, in no hurry, proceeded to hold 'court' as the local merchants arrived at the camp, bringing with them a large amount of gold and silver, as well as proposing to buy the Israelites as slaves. Perhaps the very arrogance and over-confidence implied by this event helps to explain the subsequent Seleucid defeat.

The Battle of Emmaus

Judas was aware of the strength of the army marching to 'destroy' him as he would have had it under observation as soon as it approached Judaea. However, the army of Nicanor faced him with a situation he had not yet had to confront – the need to give battle with a large, well-equipped and very powerful Seleucid army. Furthermore, the knowledge 'that the King had ordered the people's total destruction' weighed heavily on the choices open to Judas. Doubtless he was fully aware of the capacity for such a force to engage in a long campaign against him, particularly if the ruthless policy of exterminating the population destroyed the very intelligence, supply and support base on which his guerrilla army depended. Whether he liked it or not, he would have to move against the Seleucid army at the earliest possible opportunity.

Given the mood of the times and the great threat bearing down upon them the people gathered at Mizpah, the traditional rallying place of the people of Israel. There they called on the Lord for mercy and attempted to divine his will with respect to the forthcoming battle.

Again the *Books of Maccabees* are in disagreement as to the size of the force that Judas took against the Seleucids. However, we can presume that Judas was able to bring to battle at least 3000 men and perhaps as many as 6000. Whilst preferring to depend on his own guerrilla forces, on the grounds of their reliability, the size of the enemy he was up against no doubt dictated the need to impress as many men as he could into the army he was to take into the field. He must have been acutely conscious of the disparity between his own force and that of the enemy in terms not only of weaponry and equipment but also of his men's lack of experience

Maccabean infantry at Emmaus would have looked little different than when the revolt started – apart from the growing effectiveness of weapons obtained mainly from those abandoned by the Seleucids.

in open warfare. So whilst he needed numbers, he also needed a plan that would allow him to exploit his traditional guerrilla strengths of knowledge of terrain, stealth and surprise. He therefore decided to attack the Seleucid forces at Emmaus without delay.

Forming up his men, he moved northwards and took up a position some miles to the south of the Seleucid encampment at Emmaus. However, unlike his opponents in their 'settlement' of tents and large baggage train, Judas required his men to stand to arms with only a few fires to mark their presence.

It would seem then that Judas had originally intended to fight a conventional battle against the Seleucid army on the following day and that the prospects for a successful outcome were not at all promising. However, during the night something occurred that swung the whole issue in his favour. Word came back to him – no doubt from men he had detached to observe the enemy encampment – that a large force had detached itself from the main body and was heading towards Judas' encampment.

Indeed this was the case. Gorgias had decided to fall on Judas while still in his camp (clearly his position was known!) and had told Nicanor that

It was in the vicinity of Emmaus – as it appears today – that Judas Maccabeus and his army was able to inflict their first defeat on a regular Seleucid army that had been raised to destroy the rebels and suppress the Jewish rebellion.

23

he was taking 5000 foot and 1000 cavalry in order to do so. At the dead of night and led by Jewish sympathisers, the Seleucid force made their way, probably slowly on account of their unfamiliarity with and the roughness of the terrain, towards where they knew Judas to be. With a headstart, Judas struck his own camp and, leading his men rapidly over ground they knew like the back of their hand, made straight for the Seleucid encampment at Emmaus. He assumed that those in the encampment would imagine that Gorgias would rapidly destroy the Jewish forces and that they needed no assistance to do so, secure in the belief that this Jewish thorn in the flesh was even now being destroyed.

Even as Gorgias arrived at Judas' abandoned camp, and jumped to the erroneous conclusion that the Jews had withdrawn rather than fight, the Maccabean forces were drawn up in front of the Seleucid encampment at Emmaus, ready for battle.

By now it was first light and Judas was too wily a commander not to take advantage of the lowered guard and slowness of response that come with waking from sleep. With an encampment only half-awake and secure in the false knowledge that its enemy was even now being destroyed, Judas ordered the trumpets to be blown and the advance began. Panic enveloped the Seleucid camp and even though some forces managed to deploy to face the rapidly advancing Jewish line, it was to no avail. The Maccabean forces swept in and, caught totally off guard, the Seleucid forces dissolved in front of the ferocious onslaught. Fleeing for their lives, the retreat became a rout.

Victory

Judas instructed his well disciplined forces to halt the pursuit:

'Never mind the booty, for we have another battle ahead of us. First stand up to our enemies and fight them and then you can safely collect the booty'. The words were hardly out of Judas' mouth, when a detachment came into view, peering down from the mountain. Observing that their own troops had been routed and that the camp had been fired – since the smoke, which they could see attested the fact – they were panic stricken at the sight; and when, furthermore they saw Judas' troops drawn up for battle on the plain, they all fled into Philistine territory. Judas then turned back to plunder the camp, and a large sum in gold and silver, with violet and sea purple stuffs and other valuables were carried off.

(1 *Maccabees* 4:18–24)

Judas had won a remarkable victory, realised through great daring and audacity. However, the Seleucids were not about to give up their hold on Judaea and within a short time of their defeat at Emmaus they were putting together another army to destroy Judas. This time, however, the campaign was to be led and waged by Lysias himself, so alarmed had he become about the passage of events in Judaea.

At the same time, it was the make up of the opposing armies and the tactics employed that had contributed to the victories of Judas – and which was to influence the outcome of his greatest battles.

Armies and Weapons

In the six years between his assumption of the leadership of the Jewish resistance forces and his death at the battle of Elasa in 160 B.C., Judas Maccabeus was involved in almost continual warfare with the forces of the Seleucid empire. Over that period the Maccabean forces evolved from their origins as a guerrilla force into an army able to take on their Seleucid opponents in conventional battle. The Book of Maccabees constantly portrays Judas as the underdog, with small forces. This is a result of the historian of the House of Hasmon not wanting to diminish the scale or glory of the victories – and to provide an excuse for defeats. In reality there is evidence to show that the numbers of men available between 166 and 160 B.C. were considerably larger than those suggested, particularly after the re-dedication of the Temple in 164 B.C.

The Growing Army

In the early days of the rebellion the numbers of men available were very small although these rapidly grew in number as the fame of Judas spread. By the Battle of Emmaus in 164 B.C., some two years after the beginning of the rebellion, Judas was able to put 3000 men into the field.

However, the greatest increase in the size of the Maccabean army occurred after the purification of the Temple. In the expeditions into the regions around Judaea to bring back those Jews lying beyond the protection of his arms he could field at least 20,000 men, such a figure being arrived at by totalling the men despatched on the various expeditions to the areas surrounding Judaea as well as those lost in battle. The biblical image of continually small Maccabean forces taking on overwhelmingly large enemy armies and overcoming them is just not tenable.

Maccabean Weaponry

Throughout the time that Judas led the rebels the bulk of his forces were light infantry. In the early days, when functioning in a guerrilla capacity, the Maccabean forces were poorly equipped, with many of the better weapons and other equipment such as body armour being obtained as booty from the defeated Seleucid forces, just as Judas acquired his own sword from the hand of the dead Apollonius. However, by the time of Beth-Zechariah, when Judas was able to oppose the Seleucid phalanx with one of his own, the equipment would have been manufactured in the towns of Judaea as well as being brought into the province by the Jews returning from abroad.

The nearly continuous warfare in which Judas was involved, particularly after 164 B.C., must point to more sophisticated means of weapons acquisition, although the Maccabean forces on the battlefield would never have looked like the regular units of the Seleucid army. Apart from

Almost all the helmets employed by the Seleucid soldiery were variations of the Thracian type. Whilst those of officers were sometimes of iron, those of the other ranks were normally made of bronze, either left in the natural metal finish or painted.

the heavy infantry, most of the lighter units would have eschewed a uniform and retained the appearance of 'organised irregulars'. From the account in the *First Book of Maccabees* of Judas mustering his forces prior to the battle of Emmaus, the Maccabean organisation seems to have been in the traditional form, from Moses, of units of 1000 subdivided into hundreds, fifties and tens. While the text makes no mention of the Maccabean forces possessing cavalry, there is an interesting 'slip of the pen' in the *Second Book of Maccabees* in which there is mention of a horseman called Dositheus. Bar-Kochva, the eminent authority on the Seleucid army, believes that he can show fairly conclusively that Dositheus came from a Ptolemaic military settlement in the Trans-Jordan.

The Seleucid Phalanx

The core of the Seleucid armies of Antiochus IV Epiphanes, of Demetrius and of all other Seleucid monarchs, in keeping with the Hellenistic tradition in warfare, was the phalanx. Throughout the greater period of the existence of the Empire, the Seleucid kings were able to deploy on the major campaigns two corps of phalangites or phalanx troopers numbering 'some tens of thousands'. These two corps were designated either simply the 'phalanx' or the argyraspides, who were the infantry guard. These were available as a permanent force at the heart of the Empire. Whilst predominantly encountered as part of the Seleucid phalanx, the argyraspides were also employed as non-phalanx infantry, suggesting a capacity to change rôle as needs demanded.

In the light of the central role played by the phalanx, and of the heterogeneity of peoples within the Seleucid empire, it was vital for the kings to be able to draw on a large number of loyal persons to serve within the phalanx. It is not surprising therefore to discover that such troops were exclusively recruited from the ranks of military settlers living in settlements known as *katoikiai*, established by the Seleucids to provide them with a steady source of able and loyal manpower. The inhabitants of these *katoikiai*, of which there were some forty-five, were predominantly Greco-Macedonians, their descendants holding land from the King in return for the obligation to provide military service. This was a generational compact in which the sons of soldiers inherited the obligations to serve along with the land. This enabled the Seleucid kings to maintain a phalanx stable in numbers for some considerable time, even taking into account losses on campaign.

The hard core of the phalangist infantry was concentrated in settlements close to the heart of the empire around Antioch in northern Syria to allow rapid mobilisation in time of war. Such settlements also provided the horse guard and the cataphracts, and possibly some light cavalry as well. From the *katoikiai* in Asia Minor, northern Syria and Mesopotamia and the eastern provinces, of which Media was the most important, it seems that some 44,000 phalangists, 3000 semi-heavy

infantry and 8000–8500 cavalry could be raised. This marked the maximum recruitment potential rather than the actual forces deployed. At Magnesia, for example, the infantry from the settlements allowed a phalanx of 16,000 men to be deployed. However, as the Seleucid borders contracted and military settlements were lost, the numbers available for service declined.

Infantry in Action

The phalanx of Antiochus Epiphanes was, in many respects, identical to that of his predecessors but with his own innovations. Composed of chrysaspides, chalkaspides and the argyraspides, all phalangists were equipped with the huge, two-handed pike – the 7 metre-long sarissa. The shield, some 45 cm in diameter, was strapped to the left forearm allowing the 6 kilogramme sarissa to be held in both hands on the right side of the body.

The name argyraspides, meaning 'silver shields', went back to the time when Alexander issued silver shields to his hypaspists before the great battle of the Hydaspes in India. They formed a unit that retained its size at 10,000 men, recruited again from the *katoikiai* but from amongst the fittest and most able in the empire. Under Antiochus, some 5000 of the argyraspides had their traditional Macedonian panoply of heavy body armour and greaves replaced by a new uniform and equipment in the manner of the Roman triarius, except for the traditional helmet which was retained. The King hoped that by employing the more flexible Roman 'infantry' alongside the power of the phalanx he could exploit the strengths of both to his advantage. Indeed, at Beth-Zechariah it was the 'Roman' units with their mail armour who were detailed to protect the elephants in the first division moving into the defile against the Maccabean phalanx.

Apart from the phalangists, other Seleucid infantry included numbers of peltasts or thureophoroi. However, many of these troops were also recruited as mercenaries and as many as 10,000 may have served on Antiochus' expedition against the Parthians. Certainly, the Seleucids made extensive use of infantry recruited locally. These troops tended to

Little is known of the tactical organisation of the Seleucid phalanx, the core of the professional Seleucid army, though this is its probable general appearance. However, by the time of the Jewish rebellion, bitter experience at the hands of the more flexible tactical organisation of the Roman Legion meant that on the battlefield the days of the phalanx were numbered.

The phalangites, carrying their 21-foot sarissas and their shields strapped to their left arms, formed the main striking units of the field armies.

Apart from the guard cavalry, the bulk of the heavy mounted units were fitted out as cataphracts by the time of the Jewish rebellion. It was Antiochus III, following his wars against the Parthians, who converted the Seleucid cavalry into these armoured horse soldiers.

be poorly trained and poorly motivated and were just used to bolster the numbers of the field army, as at Magnesia.

Cataphracts

We have already mentioned that the regular cavalry were recruited from the military settlements. By the time of Magnesia, all the cavalry – other than the two élite guard units which numbered 1000 men – were of the heavy type known as cataphracts. The first élite cavalry unit was named 'the Companions' and was recruited from the settlements in Lydia, Syria and Phrygia. The second unit, or the Agema, was originally recruited from amongst the Medes until the area succumbed to the Parthians, after which a new Agema was recruited from the 'Macedonian' colonists. Unlike the regular cavalry, the élite units were not equipped as full cataphracts. They were described by Livy at Magnesia as having 'lighter protection for their riders and their mounts, but in other equipment not unlike the cataphracts'. The movement towards a heavy cavalry arm came in the wake of Antiochus III's experiences fighting the Parthians. They made such an impression that by the time of the Battle of Magnesia all the cavalry had been re-equipped as such. The Greek historian Polybius described their appearance as 'men and horses completely armoured'.

Elephants of War

However, the Seleucids were most famous for their use of elephants. Although by the beginning of the reign of Antiochus III only ten elephants remained from a once large herd, through trade he was able to raise the figure to 102 by 217 B.C. With additional animals secured from

Bactrian and Indian sources he was able to further increase his herd to 150. Once again, by the time of Antiochus IV the number of elephants had been drastically reduced. However, despite the treaty of Apamea, which required all elephants to be handed over to the Romans, the King still managed to take an undetermined number on his Egyptian campaign. At Daphne in 166 B.C. he paraded either 36 or 42 elephants, which probably represented the total herd available to him. Indeed, the last time that the Seleucids were to use elephants on a field of battle was during Lysias' second campaign against Judas and in the Battle of Beth-Zechariah – the appearance of the elephants probably being the determining factor in the battle, so unused were Judas' men to fighting against such creatures. In all, Lysias probably only had about eight available to him.

It is not possible to do more than sketch the make-up of the military forces of the respective combatants of this time but it was with these

Though for so long the distinctive feature of the Seleucid field armies, Beth-Zechariah marked the last occasion that the war elephant was employed by the Seleucids. Nevertheless, these animals, albeit extensively protected by shielding units, did much to shatter the Maccabean line in that battle.

forces that Maccabee and Seleucid set out to determine the fate of Judaea and the Jewish people.

Victory at Beth-Zur

In the wake of the débâcle at Emmaus, Lysias must have realised that in the person of Judas he was faced with an enemy of no mean military ability. Furthermore, his own standing and even his life may well now be in the balance once the news of Emmaus reached the ears of the King. Having decided that the only politic thing to do was to re-establish his credibility by ending the Jewish rebellion once and for all, he set about raising another army with the intention of leading the next campaign to Judaea himself.

In the short account of the first campaign of Lysias (1 *Maccabees* 4:28ff), we are faced with a description of a Seleucid army that is much too large given the forces actually available. Lysias is described as having mobilised 60,000 picked troops and 5000 cavalry with the intention

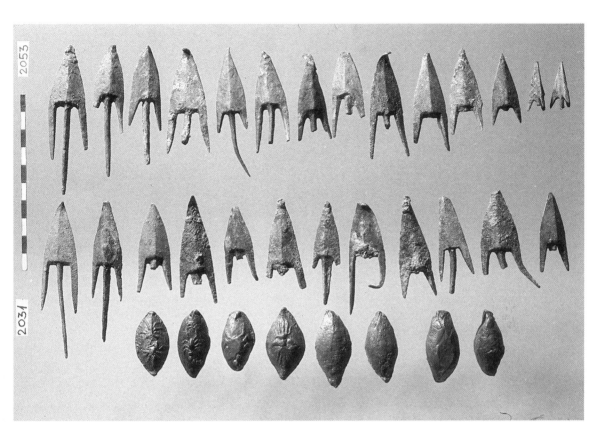

of finishing off the Jews. In the *Second Book of Maccabees* (11:2) we are presented with even larger figures – some 80,000 foot soldiers and Lysias' entire cavalry. The difficulty with either set of figures is that at this time – that is before the death of Antiochus IV – the bulk of the forces available to the Seleucids as a whole were engaged in the campaign in the east against the Parthians.

Although excavated at Acco, these Hellenistic arrowheads and slings are typical of the projectile weapons used against the defenders of Beth-Zur.

Key to Jerusalem

With his army assembled, Lysias advanced on Judaea. Learning from the lessons of the previous expeditions he deliberately avoided the obvious line of advance, which was to climb onto the Judaean plateau by way of the north or north-western passes. He was fully aware of the degree to which the Jewish population in those regions was hostile to the Seleucids, and he had no desire to present Judas with another opportunity to catch a Seleucid army strung out and vulnerable in a mountain pass. He therefore took his army by the south-western route, which allowed him to approach Jerusalem from the south after passing through the territory of the Edomaeans, who supported the Seleucids against the Jews. Both sides were aware that the key to Jerusalem was the fortress of

Beth-Zur, lying some 27 kilometres to the south of the city, and it was there that Judas had assembled his force of 10,000 men.

By all the accounts of the subsequent battle, Judas managed to defeat Lysias:

the two forces engaged, and five thousand men of Lysias' troops fell in hand to hand fighting. Seeing the rout of his army and the courage of Judas' and their readiness to live or die nobly, Lysias withdrew to Antioch.

(1 *Maccabees* 4:34–35)

Now, it is possible, given the inconsistencies in the accounts of the battle in both *Books of Maccabees* and by Josephus in the *Antiquities*, that Lysias' abandonment of the battlefield and his sudden return to Antioch may have had more to do with receiving news of the illness of Antiochus IV Epiphanes on campaign in the east. The political consequences for the succession would have been considered serious enough, with as much threat to his own position as from the results of the Battle of Beth-Zur.

For Judas, however, the abandonment of Judaea by the Seleucid army meant that the Jews could now realise their ambition to purify the Temple and re-dedicate the sanctuary in Jerusalem.

The Temple Rededicated

In the wake of Lysias' defeat at Beth-Zur, Judas determined to seize the initiative and return to Jerusalem to purge it of the pro-Seleucid and apostate Jews and purify and re-dedicate the Temple of the Lord.

With his army in tow, Judas entered the holy city and went up to Mount Zion on which stood the 'Temple'. They found the sanctuary deserted, the altar desecrated, the gates burned down, and vegetation growing in the courtyards.

Despite the dismay and anger at what he found, Judas was determined to rectify the situation. With the pro-Seleucid party effectively holed up in the Akra, he selected priests who had shown no taint of Hellenism and who were 'blameless and zealous for the Law' to begin the task of purifying the sanctuary. The act of the greatest profanity and pollution in the holiest of places was the erection of the altar to Olympian Zeus on the order of Antiochus. The altar was demolished and the stones placed in a cave on the hill of the Dwelling. The priests:

took unhewn stones, as the Law prescribed, and built a new altar on the lines of the old one. They restored the Holy Place and the interior of the Dwelling, and purified the courts. They made new sacred vessels, and brought the lamp stand, the altar of incense and the table into the Temple. They burned incense on the altar and lit the lamps on the lamp stand and these shone inside the Temple. They placed the loaves on the table and hung the curtains and completed all the tasks they had undertaken.

(1 *Maccabees* 4:47–51)

The Battle of Beth-Zechariah, where the overwhelming might of the Seleucid army defeated the Maccabean forces. Unable to withstand the enemy phalanx and supporting elephants, Judas' men fled the field.

Festival of Lights

So it was that on the 25th of the month of Chislev (December 164 B.C.) and on the third anniversary of the first sacrifice to Zeus the priests 'offered a Lawful sacrifice of burnt offering which they had made'. Then there followed eight days of celebration and festivities, the disgrace inflicted by the Seleucids having been finally effaced.

As a consequence of this event:

Judas, with his brothers and the whole assembly of Israel made it a law that the days of dedication of the altar should be celebrated yearly at the proper season, for eight days beginning on the twenty fifth of the month Chislev, with rejoicing and gladness.

(1 Maccabees 4:59)

The seven-branched candlestick called the Menorah is still used each year to commemorate Hanukkah, the Festival of Lights.

This festival is still commemorated to this day and is known in the Jewish religious calendar as The Festival of Lights or Hanukkah. In many Jewish homes, the seven-branched candlestick known as the Menorah is lit, with one candle being lit for each day of the festival. Thus the Jews of the present day keep faith with their ancestors who fought so desperately to keep their faith alive in the face of a ruthless and vindictive attempt to destroy it – truly a victory of light over darkness.

End of an Enemy

The death of Antiochus IV Epiphanes in late 164 B.C., at the time of the re-dedication of the Temple, was seen as the judgement of God on the arrogance and cruelty of this man, who had presumed to call himself a 'god' and had polluted the Temple of the Lord:

And so this murderer and blasphemer, having endured sufferings as terrible as those which he had made others endure, met his pitiable fate, and ended his life in the mountains far from his home

(2 Maccabees 9:28)

Judas followed up the death of his enemy and of the purification of the sanctuary by fortifying the Temple Mount and the strategic site of Beth-Zur. He had every reason to suppose that Lysias would return at the head of a larger army and resume the attempt to crush the revolt.

At the same time with the majority of the Seleucid forces out of Judaea, Judas took the opportunity to strike out at those in the surrounding territories who had exploited the edict of Antiochus by attacking Jews outside Judaea. Leading his armies out beyond the borders of the province for the first time, he fought successfully against the Edomaeans in the south, the 'children of Baean' and the Ammonites. This prompted the populations in Gilead and the Trans-Jordan to persecute any Jews in those areas, so Judas delegated Simon to lead a force into Galilee. Having defeated the enemy there, Simon led the Jewish families of Galilee and Arbatta and their possessions to Judaea in triumph.

An attempt to take Jamnia was defeated by the Seleucid general Gorgias, but during a second campaign against the Edomites Judas took

Lured away from the main battle at Elasa by a Seleucid stratagem, Judas and his small cavalry force were isolated and cut off by Bacchides' guards. So died the great hero, beneath the enemy lances, in 160 B.C.

The Edomaeans, against whom Judas also campaigned, were more than happy to allow the Seleucid armies transit through their territory and supplied Lysias with many auxiliary troops to attack Judaea from the south.

the ancient city of Hebron where David had once ruled as King. Pushing into the coastal plain, Judas destroyed the temples of the former Philistine city of Ashdod. With the surrounding areas pacified, he returned to Jerusalem determined to destroy forever the renegades from amongst his own people even now walled up behind the great defences of the citadel, the Akra (or Acra), on the Temple Mount.

Battle of Beth-Zechariah

It was in the winter of 163–162 B.C. that Judas began the siege of the Akra in Jerusalem. Bringing siege engines to back up the blockade, they attempted to break through the very powerful defences of the Akra, but to little avail. This was a telling tribute to the sophisticated design of Seleucid fortifications. It was also a comment on the lack of skill and expertise possessed by the Maccabean forces when it came to siege techniques.

The blockade was also not secure enough to prevent a few of the besieged from escaping. With the help of a number of renegades, these pro-Seleucids made their way to Antioch to petition Antiochus V to come to their aid.

In reality their appeal was not so much to the King – who was only nine years of age – but to Lysias who, having declared himself Regent, was the real power in the land. Lysias certainly had no desire to write off Judaea and there can be no doubting that his initial defeat by Judas at Beth-Zur still rankled. The Seleucid court was always a place of intrigue and it was important that Lysias demonstrate his power and recover his prestige. Settling finally with Judas and his 'Maccabean' rebels offered the obvious opportunity. Lysias thus once more set about the task of raising an army and one that this time would be unlikely to be bettered by the wily Jewish rebel.

The most common of the Edomaean auxiliaries were archers. Very lightly armed, apart from the compound bow, they provided the Seleucids with valuable longer range fire support.

The Forces Gather

Despite the two conflicting accounts of a total for the Seleucid army of 'a hundred thousand foot soldiers, twenty thousand cavalry and thirty two elephants' (1 *Maccabees* 6:30) and 'one hundred and ten thousand infantry, five thousand cavalry, twenty two elephants and three hundred chariots fitted with scythes' (2 *Maccabees* 13:2), a figure in the region of 50,000 infantry and 5000 cavalry, including many Edomaean and Phoenician mercenaries, is probably nearer the truth. This is supported by the historian Bar-Kochva, who also argues for a total of about eight elephants (this being the last occasion they were employed by the Seleucids) and for no chariots to have taken part at all. As he did during his first campaign, Lysias approached Judaea from the south-west

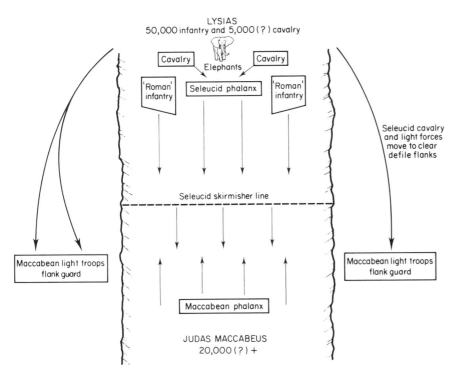

Probable disposition of the Seleucid and Maccabean forces in the defile at Beth-Zechariah, just prior to the initial clash of arms.

through Edomaean territory. His first concern before moving on to Jerusalem was to secure the fortress of Beth-Zur, the scene of his previous defeat by Judas, in order to secure his lines of communication. He thus put Beth-Zur under siege for many days with siege engines. However, the defenders made a sortie from the walls and set them on fire.

Abandoning the siege in Jerusalem, Judas called together his army and marched southwards in the direction of the Seleucids and pitched camp at Beth-Zechariah some 9 kilometres from Beth-Zur and beside the road to Jerusalem. Clearly, he was adopting a blocking position in the hope of preventing Lysias from advancing on Jerusalem.

It is uncertain whether Judas was attempting to launch a surprise attack on the advancing Seleucid forces or had drawn up his battle line in preparation for a conventional battle. However, the size of the army available to Judas was clearly quite large – in the region of some 20,000 men. This army was composed mainly of heavy and semi-heavy infantry, forming a Jewish phalanx located in the centre of the line. They would have been equipped with body armour and sarissas and supported by cavalry. This whole body was drawn up across a defile at Beth-Zechariah, with its flanks protected by the rising hills on either side with probably a screen of light units for flank protection on either slope of the defile. Such a position offered the Jewish forces the opportunity to restrict the size of the units the Seleucids could deploy and also their room for manoeuvre in the limited space in front of the defile.

Spectacle of Battle

Arriving in sight of the Jewish army, Lysias gave the command for his army to deploy in a battle line to intimidate the Maccabean forces. Strung out across the valley, the Seleucid army must have posed a magnificent spectacle – the armour, chain mail and weaponry glinting in the sunlight, the elephants with their towers surmounted with shields and the noise of thousands of men and horses as they moved into position, all set against the colour provided by shields, cloaks and pennants. If Lysias intended to inspire awe and dread by presenting the face of seeming omnipotent military power, then he may well have struck the right chord.

Simultaneously, the Seleucid force on the plain had deployed into a number of divisions of novel composition in order to begin the assault on the Maccabean line, the elephants being the focus of each division:

These animals were distributed among the phalanxes, to each elephant being allocated a thousand men dressed in coats of mail with bronze helmets on heads; five hundred picked horsemen were also assigned to each beast. The horsemen anticipated every move their elephant made; wherever it went they went with it, never quitting it. On each elephant to protect it, was a stout wooden tower, kept in position by girths, each with its three

combatants, as well as its mahout. The remainder of the cavalry was stationed on one or other of the two flanks of the army, to harass the enemy and cover the phalanxes.

(1 Maccabees 6:35–38)

In his *Jewish Antiquities* Flavius Josephus speaks of these 'self-contained units' deploying from a wide battle line into column before entering the defile to confront the Maccabean forces. Thus each unit presented to the enemy what was in itself a miniature of the battle line.

Gallantry in Defeat

From the description given in *Maccabees*, the phalanxes were equipped not with the more usual phalangites but with soldiers dressed and equipped in the Roman fashion, allowing them to respond more flexibly in the confined spaces of the defile. Screened by a line of skirmishers, the Seleucid line advanced towards the Jewish forces. It was at this point that, according to *Maccabees*, one 'Eleazar called Avran', the brother of Judas, launched himself forward into the Seleucid troops and, having cut his way through, attacked an elephant believing it to be carrying the boy King. Whilst making for good reading, the whole event is most unlikely to have occurred in the manner described, simply on the grounds that

Following the decisive defeat of the Maccabean forces at the battle of Beth-Zechariah, Judas and his followers fled to the safety of the Gophna hills, there to recuperate and await the outcome of events.

37

one man would hardly have been able to cut through so many enemy soldiers who were there specifically to protect the elephants. Nevertheless, it is very probable that there was an outstanding deed of courage by a single Jewish soldier to inspire his comrades in the face of growing defeat.

The Bible has very little to say about the course of this very important battle, perhaps because in the end it was a severe defeat for Judas and his army. It is difficult to speculate with so little evidence, but a plausible scenario is that the Seleucid forces on the hills rapidly pushed aside the Jewish units covering the flanks of the defile and exposed the Maccabean forces in the defile itself. Under growing and powerful frontal pressure in the defile itself, with the elephants generating a deep sense of unease and fear, the limited success the Maccabeans had achieved in the centre against the Seleucid skirmishers gave way. Their flanks now exposed and the enemy cavalry pushing into their rear, panic set in and the Maccabean army fled from the field, abandoning most of their equipment and leaving behind many dead and dying. Such must be inferred from the silence of the text on this matter. From Josephus we learn that, having abandoned the battlefield, Judas and his surviving followers fled to Gophna, into the hills near Bethel. The scale of the Jewish defeat now unlocked the door to Jerusalem and once again it looked to Judas that the Holy City and the Temple, so recently purified and re-dedicated was to be polluted by the presence of the gentiles.

Religious Freedom

As the news of the disastrous defeat of Judas at Beth-Zechariah reached Jerusalem, only the pro-Seleucid forces still blockaded in the Akra gave thanks. For the rest of the population, it seemed that their nemesis was coming closer with every mile that Lysias' army drew nearer the city. Many of the soldiers that survived the defeat set about preparing the city for the inevitable siege that was to follow.

With the fortress of Beth-Zur now under his control and garrisoned, Lysias could bring up the machines that formed so formidable an element in the Seleucid arsenal:

He besieged the sanctuary for a long time, erecting battering and siege engines, flame throwers and ballistas, scorpions to discharge arrows and catapults. The defenders countered these by constructing their own engines and were thus able to prolong their own resistance.

(1 *Maccabees* 6:51–53)

However, there was virtually no food in the city and starvation began to take its toll. As it was the seventh year, the 'Sabbatical Rest' in which no crops were sown, it was not possible to lay in reserves in the food stores.

Very large numbers of light skirmishing troops, like this thurephoros or peltast, were used by the Seleucids. They preceded the phalanx into battle, dispatching their javelins to unnerve and unsteady the enemy line. At Beth-Zechariah, the only Maccabean success lay in their defeat of the Seleucid skirmisher line.

38

Food shortages also affected the attackers, for there were no crops for them either, and what little there was was hidden by the hostile populace. Thus when Lysias received news that Philip – whom Antiochus Epiphanes had appointed before his death to act as Regent to his son – had returned to Antioch and was even now moving to assume power in the empire, he resolved to end the siege and the war post haste and return to Syria to protect his position.

Murder of the High Priest

In the name of the King, Lysias offered peace to the Jews on the basis of a return to the law granting them the right to freedom of worship as laid down by Antiochus III.

However, to the Seleucids the offer covered only the Temple and not the city walls, which they felt at liberty to pull down. Having retained their political authority over Judaea, it was clearly expedient to destroy the means whereby the city could hold out against them if ever the need arose in the future to quell rebellion in the province. According to Josephus, amongst the baggage and booty taken by the Seleucids when they returned to Antioch was Menelaus, the High Priest. He was put to death on the order of Antiochus V by being thrown down into a tower full of ashes, the King having been told by Lysias that Menelaus was responsible for the Seleucid woes in Judaea.

New King and New Priest

In 162 B.C. Demetrius, grandson of Antiochus III and rightful heir to the Seleucid throne, managed to escape from an enforced Roman custody with the assistance of the Greek historian and statesman Polybius. He made his way to Antioch where he was successful in wooing the army to his cause as the rightful king of the Seleucid empire. That same year he was crowned, taking the name Demetrius I Soter (Preserver).

It was the revolt against him by the Seleucid general Timarchus in Babylonia and the subsequent drawing eastwards of the bulk of Demetrius' main army to deal with the revolt that provided Judas with the opportunity to make a final bid for political freedom of his people.

Many Jews were prepared to forgo any further opposition to the Seleucid crown on the grounds that they had been granted full religious freedom. However, Judas Maccabeus felt that the Jews could never be certain that freedom to live according to their ancestral Law would not be rescinded again, unless they were politically independent of any foreign power.

Not surprisingly, a political struggle began in Judea between those who supported the Seleucids, and the others, led by Judas, who wished to continue the fight for full political independence. Naturally the Seleucids had no reason or desire to deal with Judas, and so consciously set about strengthening the Hellenising party amongst the Jews.

In 162 B.C. Demetrius, son of Seleucus IV, escaped from Rome. Returning to Antioch he procured the deaths of Lysias and Antiochus V with the help of the army. In 160 B.C., he despatched an army to Judaea under Bacchides with instructions to kill Judas Maccabeus.

When Demetrius became King in Antioch he appointed in Jerusalem a new High Priest by the name of Alcimus. Whilst Alcimus was a member of a legitimate priestly family, he was also a Helleniser. This provoked the wrath of Judas, who managed to prevent him taking up his post in Jerusalem. After appealing to the King in Antioch, Alcimus was sent back to Jerusalem escorted by an army under the generalship of Bacchides. Attempts to parley with the Maccabean forces came to nought, but on the road to Jerusalem an incident occurred that transformed the situation:

> A commission of scribes presented themselves before Alcimus and Bacchides, to sue for just terms. The first among the Israelites to ask for peace terms were the Hasidaeans who reasoned thus, 'This is a priest of Aaron's line who has come with the armed forces; he will not wrong us.' He did in fact discuss peace terms with them and gave them his oath, 'We shall not attempt to injure you and your friends'. They believed him, but he arrested sixty of them and put them to death.
>
> (1 *Maccabees* 7:12–16)

Why such an action occurred is difficult to fathom. Perhaps in this crude way Alcimus was demonstrating that he would brook no challenge to his authority. If so, it was a lamentable error.

Defeat of Nicanor

The Hasidaeans had supported Judas throughout the fight for religious freedom and had only broken with him once it was realised. Now they saw that it was not possible for their religious convictions to be reconciled with the new High Priest and the Seleucid King who supported him.

The situation disintegrated rapidly. The Hasidaeans returned to serve with Judas and he resorted to purging the countryside of any avowed supporters of the Hellenising party.

In the place of Bacchides, Demetrius sent Nicanor, who as 'one of his generals ranking as illustrious and bitter enemy of Israel' (1 *Maccabees* 7:26), brought an army to Judaea with orders to exterminate the people.

An attempt to abduct Judas failed. Judas called out his army and the Maccabean and Seleucid forces met on the battlefield of Adasa, where Nicanor was defeated and his army virtually destroyed. Having collected the spoils and booty, Judas' men cut off Nicanor's head and his right hand, which he had stretched out in a display of insolence. These gory trophies were taken and displayed within sight of Jerusalem, to the people's great acclaim.

Roman Treaty

In the brief period of peace that followed, Judas demonstrated his political acumen by entering into negotiations with the Romans to conclude a treaty. It is clear to see his thinking: if the Romans guaranteed Judaean independence, then the Seleucids would not dare to invade.

Within the context of Roman interests, such a policy was also quite advantageous. A treaty with Judaea would severely limit Seleucid power in the area – always a matter to their liking – and further divide the territory. In addition, the relationship would see Judas placed in a position of dependence on Rome.

The terms of the treaty are worth quoting:

If war comes first to Rome or any of her allies throughout her dominions the Jewish nation will take action as her ally, as occasion may require, and do it wholeheartedly. . . . In the same way, if war comes first to the Jewish nation, the Romans will support them energetically as occasion may offer.

Most important of all for Judas was the following clause that he felt must have assured the Jews of both their political as well as their religious freedom:

As regards the wrongs done to them by King Demetrius we have written to him in these terms: Why have you made your yoke lie heavy on our friends and allies the Jews? If they appeal against you again, we shall uphold their rights and make war on you by sea and land.

(1 *Maccabees* 8:24–32)

In the light of this treaty it must have been a surprise for Judas to learn that a Seleucid plan was afoot to 'seek out and finally destroy this meddlesome and perverse Jewish rebel'.

Death at Elasa

Demetrius had suppressed the Babylonian revolt of Timarchus and was now in a position to make available a large and powerful force with which to deal once and for all with Judas Maccabeus, the treaty between the Romans and the Jews notwithstanding. Believing that only by striking quickly could the problem in Judaea be solved, Demetrius summoned Bacchides to plan a strategy. For the first time the explicit objective was the full elimination of the leaders of the Jewish revolt. The intention was to paralyse the body by severing the head.

Whilst such an approach was certainly logical, Judas Maccabeus had never obliged the Seleucids by dancing to their battle tune unless absolutely necessary; Bacchides knew that he would have to draw Judas and his army out to fight on a battlefield of his choosing. The Seleucid strategos therefore selected with care not only his line of march into Judaea – eschewing all previous well trodden and familiar paths – but also the site of the battle and the tactics employed on the battlefield itself.

The lighter Maccabean cavalry as it was probably equipped at Elasa. Judas Maccabeus rode in the cavalry in the battle but would have been more extensively armoured.

New Tactics

In previous campaigns Seleucid forces had attempted to reach the

Judaean plateau either by approaching via the passes in the northern part of the province – in which case Judas had ambushed them as in the 'battles' against Apollonius and Seron – or they had approached from the south-west, having first attempted to seize the strategically placed fortress of Beth-Zur, and then marched on Jerusalem as Lysias had done some two years previously. Bacchides reasoned that it was likely that Judas would expect him to do the same. He therefore planned 'a strategy of the indirect approach', hoping to place himself and his army on the plateau before Judas realised what was happening. This is indeed what actually happened. Marshalling his army – reported in the *First Book of Maccabees* at 20,000 infantry and 2000 cavalry, figures with which Bar-Kochva generally concurs, including at most 10,000 phalangites to form a large phalanx – Bacchides took a route to the south-east. This allowed him to enter Judaea by the very difficult and tortuous path from the Jordan valley onto the plateau using an ascent that, although 21 kilometres long, allowed him to debouch his army in one piece and safe onto the plateau in less than a day's march. This stratagem totally outwitted Judas who was unable to act quickly enough. Judas' failure to anticipate this move was largely due to lack of intelligence: the line of march taken by the Seleucid strategos had the added advantage of moving through sparsely settled Jewish territory with very few eyes and ears with which to report to the Maccabean leader.

Now firmly ensconced on the plateau, Bacchides declined to move on Jerusalem and began a series of manoeuvres designed to gain control of the area and force Judas out to battle on a 'field' that would allow the Seleucids to effectively deploy their powerful phalanx. It would seem that he achieved this in part by resorting to a deliberate policy of terror in those territories under his army's immediate jurisdiction.

Bacchides was aware that there were those in the Jewish ranks who would be content to settle for less than political independence if religious freedom was assured by the Seleucids. He also knew that Judas needed to move quickly before the campaign dragged on and the people's support and willingness to fight the Seleucids began to flag. Thus, Bacchides was certain that Judas could not afford to stand by and watch as Jewish lives were wasted by his men. He was appealing both to Judas' heart and head in enticing him to battle, and the appeal was successful.

Myth of Battle

According to the account of the battle in the *First Book of Maccabees*, Judas marched to do battle with Bacchides with a force of some 3000 'picked' men. The Jewish forces established their camp at Elasa, with about a kilometre separating the two forces. The account then explains that on seeing the huge size of the enemy forces, the Jewish forces were terrified and many slipped out of camp, until no more than 800 remained.

Finding he had so few men left and 'with battle now inevitable' the

Lighter Seleucid cavalry units employed for scouting, devoid of body armour and equipped with minimal weaponry.

account explains how Judas had no choice but to fight. Furthermore, Judas' harangue to his men before the battle seems to smack of a *post factum* justification of the defeat to come, tailored with the benefit of hindsight: 'Up! let us face the enemy; we may yet have the strength to fight them.' Then comes a rejection of the demand by his men for a retreat, and an appeal by Judas not to dishonour themselves – and, if necessary, accept that the end was near.

This is all very out of keeping with what we have seen of Judas' character. Whilst certainly no coward, he had not survived for so long by courting death on the battlefield if he could depart and fight another day, as after Beth-Zechariah. There would seem little reason to suppose that he had changed. Indeed his earlier defeat of Nicanor must have made him optimistic about his ability to carry the day at Elasa.

The whole incident, dependent as it is on the acceptance of only 800 men being left, seems to have been a product of the historian seeking to justify Judas' defeat without detracting from his glory.

There would seem little reason to accept 800 troops being all that Judas could bring to battle. There is the indirect evidence that the Maccabean forces possessed heavy troops and a phalanx, and clearly Judas was able

The Seleucid cavalry who brought about the deaths of Judas and his men away from the battlefield of Elasa were probably units of the guard cavalry with whom Bacchides was serving at the time.

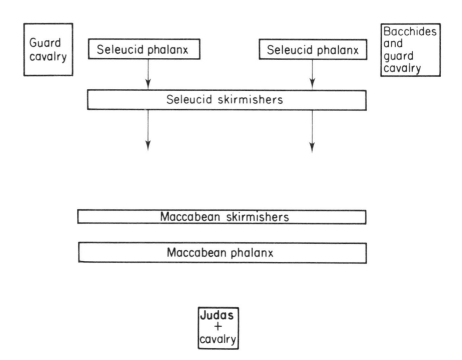

| Guard cavalry | Seleucid phalanx | | Seleucid phalanx | Bacchides and guard cavalry |

Seleucid skirmishers

Maccabean skirmishers

Maccabean phalanx

Judas + cavalry

The Battle of Elasa with the forces drawn up (above) *and in progress* (opposite) *on the assumption that Bacchides gave battle specifically to draw Judas away from the main action to his death.*

to deploy cavalry at Elasa and was himself fighting on that day from horseback.

Similarly it is from the Biblical text's silence about the composition of the Maccabean forces, allied to the absurd claims about its small size, that we get an idea as to the motivation of the historian.

One final small observation concerning the Maccabean forces is in the end the most telling. We are led to believe that, on a battlefield of their own choosing, some of the best soldiers in the Seleucid army, including at the most some 10,000 phalangites, took from 'morning until evening' (1 *Maccabees* 9:13) to defeat this small force of 800 Maccabeans.

To render this battle more credible, we must assume a considerably larger Maccabean force comprised of heavy troops forming a phalanx, and supported by light forces with cavalry. We will also now proceed on the assumption that Judas gave battle willingly, seeing no reason to fear the outcome.

Reality and Tragedy

On the morning of the battle, Bacchides assembled his force in the conventional Seleucid battle line. The heavy troops were drawn up in two divisions, forming two phalanxes each about 4000 strong. The cavalry were on the wings with a predominance being given to the right

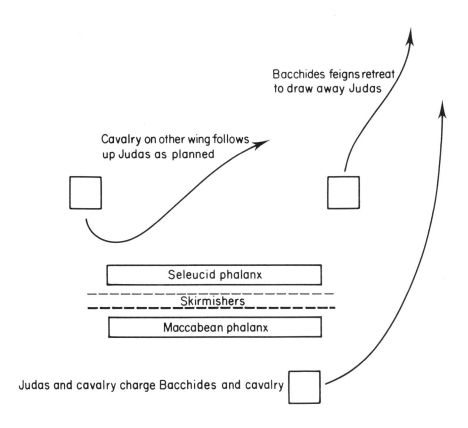

Bacchides feigns retreat
to draw away Judas

Cavalry on other wing follows
up Judas as planned

Seleucid phalanx

Skirmishers

Maccabean phalanx

Judas and cavalry charge Bacchides and cavalry

in which Bacchides himself was serving. The whole line was screened by as many as 10,000 skirmishers and it was they who closed with the Maccabean line first. Following behind the screen, the phalanx advanced in its two divisions and clashed with its Maccabean counterpart. The cavalry were held back in accordance with what seems to have been a predetermined plan to draw the Maccabean cavalry, including Judas, away from the field of battle.

At this point Judas, seeing Bacchides, launched his own cavalry at the Seleucid right wing. He was trying to repeat the tactic that had succeeded against Nicanor, whose army had disintegrated once the commander was killed. Seeing the enemy charge, the much more experienced and better trained Seleucid cavalry wheeled about and began to ride away from the field of battle, giving the impression to Judas and his men that they were retreating. After watching the Jewish cavalry follow their comrades, the left wing of the Seleucid cavalry also wheeled away from the battle line and gave full chase to Judas and his men. It was nearly 12 kilometres from the field of battle and well away from any Maccabean support that the Seleucid cavalry turned their horses and charged at Judas and his men. It was probably only then, as the left wing of the Seleucid cavalry hove into view in their rear, that Judas realised what had happened.

There was no way out. After six years of humiliating their armies and imposing on them a string of defeats, the Seleucids now had Judas Maccabeus in their grasp. Caught between two fires, the Maccabean troopers and their leader paid the enemy dear before they were speared from their horses with the long lances of the Seleucid troopers. Abandoning the bodies of Judas and his men, the Seleucid cavalry rode back to Elasa to help the phalanx defeat the remaining Maccabean forces. No doubt the Maccabean line wavered and finally broke as the Seleucid cavalry announced the death of Judas to their comrades. So fell a most remarkable man.

After the Hammer

The Bible itself records the burial of Judas and the reaction of the people he had done so much to save:

Jonathan and Simon took their brother Judas and buried him in his ancestral tomb at Modein. All Israel wept and mourned him deeply and for many days they repeated this dirge, 'what a downfall for the strong man, the man who kept Israel safe!' The other deeds of Judas, the battles he fought, the exploits he performed, and all his titles to greatness have not been recorded; but they were very many.

(1 *Maccabees* 9:19–22)

Judas Maccabeus had not lived to realise his dream of a homeland for his people, free from the political domination of the Seleucid empire. However, the mantle of striving to achieve such an end to ensure that the Jews would never again find their religious identity under threat was inherited by his brother Jonathan and, following his death, their brother Simon. It was not until 142 B.C., some eighteen years after the death of the 'Hammer' at Elasa that Simon finally forced the capitulation of the Akra in Jerusalem on the 23rd day of the Jewish month of Iyyar. Thus it was Simon, of the House of Hasmon, who made the Jews independent of the Seleucids: 'thus was the yoke of the heathen taken away from Israel'.

The grateful people of Judaea conferred upon Simon and his descendents permanent authority as the ruling High Priests of Israel.

The first foreign power to congratulate Simon and recognise him as a legitimate independent ruler and friend was the Senate of the Roman people. How ironic, therefore, that it was these same Romans who less than eighty years later brought to a close Judaea's brief independence when the clump of boots on the cobblestones of Jerusalem's streets heralded the arrival of the legions of Pompey the Great and the beginning of a domination that was to last for centuries.

Chronology of Events

301 B.C. Palestine comes under the rule of the Ptolemies of Egypt.

202 B.C. Fifth Syrian War with Seleucids under Antiochus III.

198 B.C. Palestine passes to Seleucid control; Anthiochus III confirms religious freedom of Jewish people.

190 B.C. Following disastrous attempt to invade Greece in 192 B.C., Antiochus III defeated decisively by Romans at Battle of Magnesia.

188 B.C. Treaty of Apamea; Romans force Antiochus III to give up all territories in Asia Minor west of Taurus Mountains; massive war indemnity of 15,000 talents imposed, repayable over 12 years; Antiochus III forced to send third son, Antiochus, to Rome as a hostage.

187 B.C. Antiochus III killed in Elam attempting to rob temple to help pay war indemnity; Seleucus IV succeeds to Seleucid throne.

177 B.C. Seleucus forced to send his second son Demetrius to Rome in place of Antiochus; released Antiochus makes his way to Athens.

175 B.C. Seleucus IV is assassinated; Antiochus seizes throne from usurper Heliodorus; declares himself King Antiochus IV.

174 B.C. Antiochus replaces Onias by Jason as Jewish High Priest; Jason sets out to 'Hellenize' Judaism; secures by bribery royal assent to built gymnasium in Jerusalem.

172 B.C. Jason ousted by Menelaus through payment of larger bribe to Antiochus.

169 B.C. Antiochus assumes further title Theos Epiphanes ('god manifest'); invades Egypt but forced to retreat and return to Antioch; insurrection in Jerusalem; Seleucid soldiers carry out massacre; Temple plundered with help of Menelaus.

168 B.C. Invades Egypt again; forced to retire under threat from Rome; Apollonius sent to Jerusalem to suppress further insurrection; massacres, and city walls demolished; fortress 'Akra' constructed to shelter pro-Hellenist Jews and Seleucids.

167 B.C. Antiochus orders proscription of Jewish faith; all Jewish rituals and practices forbidden on pain of death; in December orders image of Olympian Zeus erected in Temple. Harsh persecution begins.

166 B.C. Mattathias raises flag of revolt; takes to hills with sons to fight guerrilla war against Seleucids and apostate Jews; Hasidim join the rebels; Mattathias succeeded by third son Judas; Judas defeats Seleucid forces of Apollonius; Seron's force defeated at Beth-Horon.

165 B.C. Judas defeats large Seleucid army at Emmaus.

164 B.C. Lysias defeated by Judas at Beth-Zur; returns to Jerusalem rededicating Temple; Antiochus IV dies campaigning against Parthians.

163 B.C. Judas campaigns in territories surrounding Judaea to liberate Jews under persecution from Seleucid supporters; unsuccessful attempt to take Akra by siege; Lysias and boy king Antiochus V invade Judaea; major battle at Beth-Zechariah; the Maccabean army vanquished; Seleucid siege of Jerusalem abandoned after attempted coup in Antioch forces Lysias to return; decree of 167 B.C. repealed; religious freedom guaranteed; city walls destroyed; Menelaus executed.

162 B.C. Demetrius returns from Rome; kills Lysias and Antiochus V; becomes Demetrius I; Alcimus made High Priest.

161 B.C. Alcimus returns to Jerusalem with soldiers under Bacchides; killing of 60 Hasidim causes new rebellion; Judas defeats and kills Nicanor at Adasa; concludes treaty of 'Friendship and Alliance' with the Romans.

160 B.C. Demetrius despatches army to Judaea under Bacchides; Judas Maccabeus killed at Battle of Elasa.

Bibliography

Anderson, B. *The Living World of the Old Testament* Longman, 1976.

Bar-Kochva, B. *The Seleucid Army* Cambridge University Press, 1976.

Bright, J. *A History of Israel*, 3rd Edition, Philadelphia, 1981.

Ferrill, A. *The Origins of War* Thames and Hudson, 1986.

Filson, F.V. *A New Testament History* SCM, 1964.

Grant, M. *The History of Ancient Israel*, Weidenfeld & Nicolson, 1984.

Grant, M. *The Ancient Mediterranean* Weidenfeld & Nicolson, 1969.

Head, D. *Armies of the Macedonian and Punic Wars*, Wargames Research Group, 1982.

Humble, R. *Warfare in the Ancient World* Cassell BCA, 1980.

Jagersma, J. *A History of Israel from Alexander the Great to Bar-Kochva* SCM, 1985.

Noth, M.A. *History of Israel* SCM, 1958.

Pfeiffer, R. *History of New Testament Times* A. & C. Black, 1963.

Pritchard, J. (ed) *The Times Atlas of the Bible* Times Books, 1987.

Russell, D.S. *The Meaning and Message of Jewish Apocalyptic* SCM, 1964.

Index

Page numbers in *italics* refer to illustrations

Illustrations

Colour plates by Richard Hook
Line illustrations by Suzie Hole
Maps and diagrams by Chartwell Illustrators
Photographs and other illustrations courtesy of: The British Museum (pages 6, 7, 8, 9 and 39); The Jewish Education Bureau (page 33); Zev Radovan (pages 13, 21, 23, 30, 31 and 37).